I LOVE ISLAM

 International Edition

1

SCHOOL

ISLAMIC STUDIES TEXTBOOK SERIES - LEVEL ONE

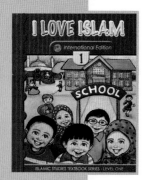

I Love Islam 1

International Edition

بسم الله الرحمن الرحيم

In the Name of Allah, Most Compassionate, Most Merciful

I Love Islam © is a series of Islamic Studies textbooks that gradually introduces Muslim students to the essentials of their faith. It brings to light the historic and cultural aspects of Islam. The series covers levels one through five, which are suitable for young learners and includes student textbooks and workbooks as well as teacher and parent's guides.

The Islamic Services Foundation is undertaking this project in collaboration with Brighter Horizons Academy in Dallas, Texas. Extensive efforts have been made to review the enclosed material. However, constructive suggestions and comments that would enrich the content of this work are welcome.

All praise is due to Allah (God), for providing us with the resources that have enabled us to complete the first part of this series. This is an ongoing project, and it is our sincere wish and hope that it will impact our Muslim children today, and for many years to come.

Copyright © 2017 by Islamic Services Foundation

ISBN 1-933301-10-5

PROGRAM DIRECTOR *

Nabil Sadoun, Ed.D.

WRITING TEAM

Aimen Ansari
Nabil Sadoun, Ed.D.
Majida Yousef

REVIEWERS AND ADVISORS

Susan Douglass
Freda Shamma, Ph.D.

CONTRIBUTORS

Isam Alimam
Ummukulthum Al-Maawiy
Lana Baghal Dasti
Suzy Fouad
Nicholas Howard
Bushra Zawi
Menat Zihni

CURRICULUM DESIGN

Majida Salem
Nabil Sadoun, Ed.D.

GRAPHIC DESIGN

Mohammed Asad

ILLUSTRATIONS

Sujata Bansal
Ramendranath Sarkar
Special thanks to:
Goodword Books

ISLAMIC SONGS AND POEMS

Noor Saadeh
NoorArt Inc.

PHOTOGRAPHY

Al-Anwar Designs
Isam Alimam

PUBLISHER AND OWNER

ISF PUBLICATIONS

Islamic Services Foundation
P.O. Box 451623
Garland, Texas 75045
U.S.A
Tel: +1 972-414-5090
Fax: +1 972-414-5640
www.myislamicbooks.com

MY BELOVED GOD

MY GREAT PROPHET

WORSHIPING ALLAH

MY MUSLIM WORLD

MY MUSLIM MANNERS

I Love Islam Friends and Family

Zaid

Leena

Mr. Mahmood

Mrs. Mahmood

Bilal

Sarah

Mr. Siraj

Mrs. Siraj

Amir

Omar

Mona

Khalid

Ahmad

Teacher Hibah

Baby Yousuf

MY BELOVED GOD

Allah, Our Great Creator

questions?

1 Have you ever seen a star shining in the night sky?
2 What has Allah created?
3 Who makes eyeglasses and cameras?
4 Who made your eyes?
5 Who made the Earth as a home for all living things?

word watch

Allah	اللّه
SubhanAllah	سُبحانَ اللّه
Masjid	مَسْجِدْ
Masajid	مَساجِدْ
Al-Khaliq	الخَالِقْ
Al-Musawwir	المُصَوّرْ
Al-Bari'	البَارِيء
MashaAllah	مَا شاءَ الله
dua'a	دُعاءْ

A toy maker made this beautiful toy.

A builder made this nice house.

Who made the world?

When we look at the Earth, the sky, mountains, animals, and people, we know that they were all created by Allah, the only Creator.

"Allah" is the Arabic word for God.
It means: *The one God we worship.*

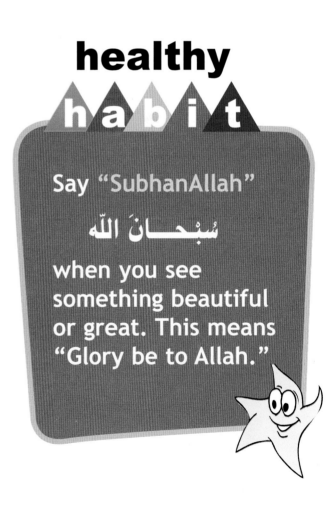

healthy
h a b i t

Say "SubhanAllah"

سُبْحانَ اللّه

when you see something beautiful or great. This means "Glory be to Allah."

Allah **is** Al-Khaliq

الخالقُ

THE CREATOR

He created the Earth for us to live on.

He created the sun to give us light and warmth during the day.

He also made the moon to give us light during the night.

"وجعلنا من الماء كل شيء حي"

WE ALL NEED WATER TO LIVE. ALLAH GAVE US WATER TO DRINK AND TO CLEAN OUR-SELVES.

WATER

The most perfect drink for all living things.

ALLAH GAVE US EVERYTHING WE NEED TO LIVE.

He gave us the **soil** to grow **food**.

He gave us **homes** to live in.

He gave us **friends** and **family** so that we do not feel lonely.

Allah (is) Al-Musawwir

المُصَوِّرُ

THE SHAPE-MAKER

Allah made the world beautiful for us.

Allah also helps us make many useful things.

■ houses
■ cars
■ schools
■ **masajid** (more than one masjid)
■ clothes
■ food

He gave us brains to use when making good things.

Everything we see is a gift from Allah.

He gave us metals to use when making cars.

He gave us wood, metals and other building materials to use when making houses and buildings.

He gave us wools, cotton and materials to use when making clothes.

healthy h a b i t

When you see pretty flowers and plants, be careful not to ruin them. Let others enjoy their beauty, too.

ACTIVITY time

Say "Subhana Allah" every time you see something beautiful or great that Allah made for us.

healthy h a b i t

When you look in the mirror and see that God has given you a good face and body, say this dua'a:

"اللّهم حَسّنْ خُلُقي كما حَسّنت خَلْقي"

"Allahuma hassin khuluqi kama hassanta khalqi"

It means: "Oh Allah, give me good manners as you have given me a perfect body"

NASHEED Allah my Creator
Listen to this nasheed and try to memorize it.

s t u d y

questions

1 Name five things Allah has given us so that we can live.

2 What should you do when you see a beautiful thing?

3 What are the Arabic names for Allah that mean "The Creator," "The Inventor" and "The Shape Maker?"

4 Say the dua'a you say when you see yourself in the mirror.

Searching for Allah

questions?

1 Can we worship the sun or the moon?
2 Can we pray to pictures or images?
3 Who was Prophet Ibraheem عليه السلام searching for?

word watch

Ibraheem   إِبْراهِيمْ

This is a story about our beloved Prophet Ibraheem عليه السلام . He was searching for God.

Let's see what happened.

Ibraheem

was a young man in Iraq.

He was looking for God.

At night, he saw a shining star. It was the biggest and brightest star in the sky.

He thought, "This must be God."

Then the star went away!

Ibraheem عليه السلام knew that God would never go away. So Ibraheem عليه السلام said, "The star is not God."

Then he saw the moon and said, "This is my God."

Then the moon disappeared.

Ibraheem عليه السلام knew the moon was not God, because God would never go away.

Ibraheem عليه السلام saw the sun in the morning, and said, "This is God."

But in the evening, the sun set and went away, too.

Ibraheem عليه السلام knew that **the sun could not be God.**

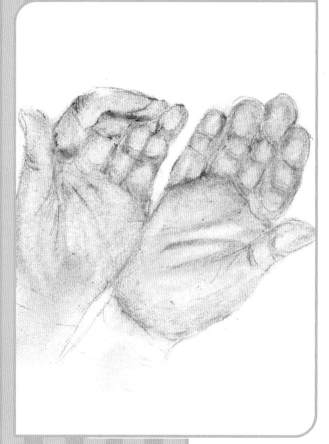

Ibraheem asked Allah to guide him.

Allah listened to Ibraheem.

Allah made Ibraheem a prophet.

healthy habit

Always worship Allah alone, do not worship anyone or anything else.

ACTIVITY time

Collect (or draw) pictures of things that remind you that Allah is "Al-Khaliq." Stick them on a poster and write "Allah is Al-Khaliq" at the top.

study questions

1 Why did Ibraheem think the star was God?

2 How did he know that the star, the moon and the sun were not God?

3 What did Ibraheem do when he could not find God?

4 Who listened to Ibraheem?

5 What did Ibraheem become?

CHAPTER 3

God is One

questions?

1. What is special about Allah?
2. Why is God only One?
3. How is Allah different from us?

word watch

Shahadah شَهَادَة
Tawheed تَوْحِيدْ
Al-Asmaa'-ul-Husna الأسْماءْ الـحُسْنى

There are five pillars of Islam.

The first pillar of Islam is the Shahadah. It is the most important thing that Muslims believe in.

In the Shahadah, Muslims say:

لا إله إلا اللّه مُحَمَّدٌ رَسولُ اللّه

"There is no God but Allah. Muhammad is the messenger of Allah."

The first part of the Shahadah says we believe in one God. The belief in one God is called Tawheed.

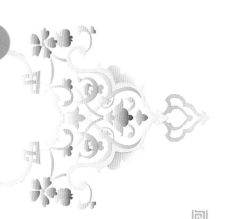

WORDS OF WISDOM

Holy Qur'an

سورة الإخلاص

Surat-ul-Ikhlas

﴿ قُلْ هُوَ ٱللَّهُ أَحَدٌ ۞ ٱللَّهُ ٱلصَّمَدُ ۞ لَمْ يَلِدْ وَلَمْ يُولَدْ ۞ وَلَمْ يَكُن لَّهُۥ كُفُوًا أَحَدٌ ۞ ﴾

TRANSLITERATION

[1] Qul huw-Allahu ahad
[2] Allah-us-samad
[3] Lam yalid walam yoolad
[4] Walam yakul lahu kufuwan ahad

TRANSLATION

[1] Say: "God is the one and only God.
[2] Allah needs no one, but all need Him.
[3] He has no child, nor was He born.
[4] And no one is like Him."

Listen to the recitation of this sura, recite it and memorize it.

Leena asked her mother one day: "Mama, why is Allah only one?"

Mama: God is One because no one can be like Him or does what He can do.

Mama: God is only One because there is nothing else like Him. Allah has all the power. No one can be like Him. No one can create the world, the stars, and the sun other than Allah. No one can make people and animals like He can.

Allah has always been here and He will always be here, forever.
He was never born and He will never die.
He does not have a mother or a father.
He does not have any children.
Allah never needs anyone to take care of Him.
He never needs any help.
There is only One God, whom we love and worship.

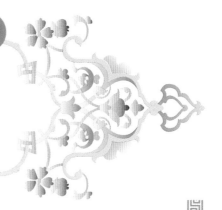

WORDS OF WISDOM
Hadeeth Shareef

حديث شريف

Narrated By At-Tirmithi

عن جابر بن عبدالله رضي الله عنه: ⸢قال رسول الله ﷺ :

رواه الترمذي   "أفضل الذكر لا إله إلا الله"

TRANSLITERATION

"Afdal-u-Thikri La Ilaha IllAllah"

TRANSLATION

Jabir Ibn Abdullah reported that the Prophet ﷺ said:
"The best way to remember Allah is to say:
"La ilaha illAllah"; there is no God but Allah.

healthy
habit

Say: ''لا إله إلا الله''

"La ilaha illAllah"

We say this as many times as we can.

Allah is One!

Allah has **Al-Asmaa-ul-Husna**, the beautiful names of Allah.
There are 99 names. Let us learn some of them:

Allah	is	Al-Wahid	الواحد ➡	The One
Allah	is	As Samad	الصمد ➡	The Self-Sufficient
Allah	is	Al-Hayy	الحي ➡	The Living
Allah	is	Al-Qayyum	القيوم ➡	The Self-Existing
Allah	is	Al-Aliyy	العلي ➡	The Most High
Allah	is	Al-Atheem	العظيم ➡	The Great

لا إله إلا الله

"La ilaha illAllah"

ACTIVITY time

With your friend, make a banner that says:

"لا إله إلا الله"

Hang it on your classroom wall.

"Shahadah"
Listen to this nasheed and try to memorize it.

study

questions

1 What do we say in the Shahadah?

2 What is the best way to remember Allah?

3 What are some names of Allah?

I Love God, He Loves Me

questions?

1. Who loves you even more than your parents?
2. How do you know that Allah loves you?
3. Why should you love Allah?
4. How much do you love Allah?

word watch

Al-Wadood الوَدودْ

I love Allah because He loves me and He gave me life.

I love Allah because He gave me eyes to see things that I love.

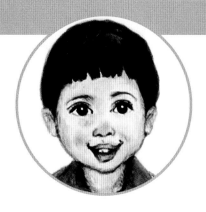

He gave me a nose to smell wonderful things.

Allah gave me ears to hear all kinds of wonderful sounds.

He gave me a mouth to smile, talk, and laugh. I also use my mouth to eat and drink.

A25

Allah gave me the sense of touch. I can feel soft and smooth things. I can feel cool and I can feel warm.

I love Allah because He loves me and He takes care of me.

Allah gave me parents and teachers to teach me good things.

He gave me a house to live in, clothes to wear, and food to eat.

Allah gave me water to drink and to clean myself.

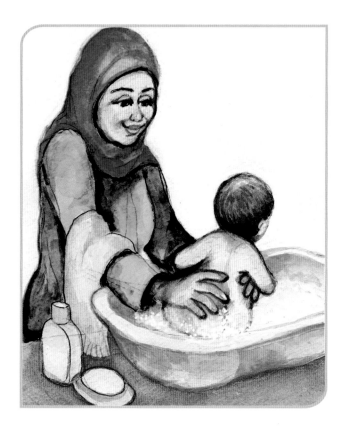

He gave me friends to
laugh, learn, and play with.

Allah gave me
family
and friends.

I Love God, He Loves Me

I love God, He loves me,
I love God, He loves me,
He is our loving lord
He is also Al-Wadood

I love God, He loves me,
He gave me my family
He created me and you,
He made us from head to toe

I love God, He loves me,
He gave me my eyes to see
He gave me my tongue to talk
and gave me my feet to walk

I love God, He loves me,
He gave me all things I need
He gave us all kinds of food
We should always make sujood

He is also Al-Wadood

I love Allah because He loves me and He made me a Muslim!

ALLAH is Al-Wadood

الوَدودُ

THE LOVING

Al-Wadood means the One that is loving. People love Allah and He loves them.

Show Allah that you love Him by doing good things. He will show you that He loves you by giving you gifts in this life and Jannah (Paradise) in the next life, inshaAllah.

healthy
habit

Always remember what Allah has given you. Learn to love Him by being a good Muslim! Always say this dua'a:

"اللهم ارزقني حبك وحب من أحبك"

"Oh Allah make me love you, and love everyone who loves you."

ACTIVITY time

1. Make a colorful drawing of the name of Allah in Arabic.

2. Make a colorful drawing of the name of Allah in English.

"I LOVE ALLAH"
Listen to this nasheed and try to memorize it.

study questions

1 Name some things Allah has given us to be thankful for.

2 We can never count how many things Allah has given us. Can you name some more things that are not in this lesson?

3 How can we show Allah that we love Him?

4 How do we know that Allah loves us?

Thank You Allah

questions?

1. Who made you? Who gave you a family? Who gave you friends?
2. Who do you always remember when you see something special?
3. Do you thank Allah for everything that you see, hear, smell, touch, and taste?
4. What is the best way to thank Allah?

word watch

Ni'mah	نعمة
Alhamdulillah	الحَمْدُ لله
Thikr	ذِكر
Al-Hameed	الحميد

Allah gave us eyes so that we can see.

Allah gave us a nose to smell and breathe with.

Allah gave us ears to hear and enjoy beautiful sounds.

Allah gave us skin so we can feel things.

Allah gave us a mouth so we can speak, taste, and smile.

These are all gifts and blessings, or **ni'mah**, from Allah.

Everything God has made is for us to use.

He wants us to be happy.

ACTIVITY time

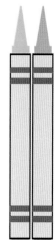

Blink!! Breathe!! Clap!! Smile!!

Now thank Allah that you can do these things.
He has given us the 5 senses.

With our eyes, we see the beautiful world. We see our loved ones, and we see things that we learn about.

With our ears, we hear Al-Qur'an, our teachers, our friends, and also nasheed.

With our mouths, we speak to each other, eat, and also breathe.

With our hands and legs we work and can feel soft, or smooth, or sticky things.

What would we do without these gifts from Allah?

We must always, always thank Him for them.

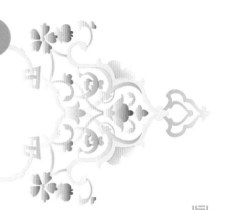

WORDS OF WISDOM

Holy Qur'an

سورة الفاتحة

Surat-ul-Fatiha

This surah is the Opening of the Qur'an. We say it to praise Allah and ask Him for guidance.

بِسۡمِ ٱللَّهِ ٱلرَّحۡمَٰنِ ٱلرَّحِيمِ ﴿١﴾ ٱلۡحَمۡدُ لِلَّهِ رَبِّ ٱلۡعَٰلَمِينَ ﴿٢﴾ ٱلرَّحۡمَٰنِ ٱلرَّحِيمِ ﴿٣﴾ مَٰلِكِ يَوۡمِ ٱلدِّينِ ﴿٤﴾ إِيَّاكَ نَعۡبُدُ وَإِيَّاكَ نَسۡتَعِينُ ﴿٥﴾ ٱهۡدِنَا ٱلصِّرَٰطَ ٱلۡمُسۡتَقِيمَ ﴿٦﴾ صِرَٰطَ ٱلَّذِينَ أَنۡعَمۡتَ عَلَيۡهِمۡ غَيۡرِ ٱلۡمَغۡضُوبِ عَلَيۡهِمۡ وَلَا ٱلضَّآلِّينَ ﴿٧﴾

TRANSLITERATION

[1] Bismillah-ir-Rahman-ir-Raheem
[2] Al-hamdu lillahi rabb-il-aalameen
[3] Ar-Rahman-ir-Raheem
[4] Maliki yawm-id-deen
[5] Iyyaka na'budu wa-iyyaka nasta'een
[6] Ihdinas-sirat-al-mustaqeem
[7] Sirat allatheena an'amta alayhim ghayr-il-maghdoobi
   alayhim walad-daalleen

TRANSLATION

[1] In the Name of Allah, The Kind, The Merciful.
[2] All praise is for Allah, Lord of the worlds.
[3] The Kind, The Merciful.
[4] King of the Day of Judgment.
[5] It is You we worship and You we ask for help.
[6] Guide us to the straight path.
[7] The path of those You have blessed, not those who have
   deserved your anger and those who have gone astray.

Listen to the recitation of this sura, recite it and memorize it.

Things we can do to thank Allah:

- Say AlhamduLillah and make dua'a

- Take care of our bodies and all that He has given us

- Pray on time, five times a day

- Obey Allah, and do everything He wants us to do

Allah is Al-Hameed

الحَميدَ

The Praiseworthy

Allah has given us every thing we have.
We must always praise Him for every (gift) ni'mah He has given us.

healthy habit

Say الحَمْدُ لله "Alhamdulillah" when you remember something Allah has created or made for us.

It means: *"All praise is for Allah."*

Praising Allah

- **Thikr** is one way to thank Allah and remember Him.

- Thikr is done by the heart and the tongue.

- Saying "SubhanAllah, **Alhamdulillah**, La ilaha illAllah, and Allahu Akbar," are kinds of thikr.

THIKR

SubhanAllah.
We praise Allah.

Alhamdulillah.
We thank Allah.

La ilaha illAllah
There is no god but Allah.
Allah is One.

Allahu Akbar.
Allah is Great.

Listen to this nasheed and try to memorize it.

 time

1. Choose a partner and look at each other's hands, eyes, mouths, and noses. Talk about these perfect creations that Allah has given us.

2. Do the following things with your friends:
- Try to use one hand in taking your notebook out of your backpack and write "Allah."
- Try to draw a house with your eyes closed.
- Try to ask your friend to give you something without speaking.

Talk about how you feel doing these things, and be thankful to Allah that He has given you hands, eyes, and a mouth.

3. Listen to this nasheed: "Thank you Allah."

 questions

1 Name something that Allah has given you that means a lot to you, something that you really love and thank Allah for. Draw it.

2 What is thikr? Give some examples.

3 How do you thank Allah?

MY GREAT PROPHET

His Name was Muhammad

questions?

1. Who was the last prophet?
2. What city did he live in when he was a boy?
3. How much should you love the Prophet?

word watch

Muhammad	مُحَمَّد
Makkah	مكة
Madina	المدينة

One day, Zaid was reading a book. It was about the last Prophet.

Zaid's mom walked into the room.

Mama: What are you reading, Zaid?
Zaid: I am reading a book about the last Prophet.
Mama: Masha'Allah Zaid! Tell me about him.
Zaid: Well, his name was Muhammad ﷺ .
Mama: Sallallahu 'alayhi wasallam.

His name was Muhammad

healthy
h a b i t

Always say

صلّى اللّهُ علیْهِ وسَلَّم

"sallAllahu 'alayhi wasallam"
when you hear the Prophet's name.

This means: 'Peace and blessings be upon him.'

Zaid: Allah chose Muhammad to be the last Prophet. Prophet Muhammad taught us good things. He showed us how to be excellent Muslims.

Mama: Yes! Prophet Muhammad ﷺ is the best example for all of us to follow.

Zaid: I love Prophet Muhammad! I want to be like him!

Mama: Where did Prophet Muhammad ﷺ live?

Zaid: He lived in **Makkah** when he was a boy. The people of Makkah loved him. Later, when he moved to **Madinah**, people there loved him, too!

Mama: We should love Prophet Muhammad ﷺ too, even more than ourselves!!!

Prophet Muhammad ﷺ was:

Patient
Honest
Wise
Kind

ACTIVITY time

1. Write the name of Prophet Muhammad ﷺ in Arabic and English.
2. Put your finger on Makkah and Madinah in the map below.

"MUHAMMAD ﷺ "

Listen to a nasheed about Prophet Muhammad and try to memorize it.

study

— questions —

1 What should you say when you hear the Prophet's ﷺ name?

2 Can you find Makkah on the map?

3 How did the people in Makkah feel about the Prophet when he was a boy?

4 Tell us about the manners of Muhammad ﷺ ?

Muhammad as a Child

questions?

1. Where was Muhammad ﷺ born?
2. Who were his parents?
3. Who were some of his uncles?
4. Who were some of his cousins?

word watch

Aminah	آمِنَـة
Abdullah	عَبْدُالله
Haleemah	حَلِيمَة
Abdul-Muttalib	عَبْدُالمُطَّلِبْ
Abu-Talib	أبو طالِبْ
Ali	عَلِي
Quraysh	قُرَيْشْ

He was born in Makkah,
where he lived most of his life.

His father was Abdullah

So his name was Muhammad Ibn Abdullah مُحمد بن عبدالله

His mother was Aminah

His grandfather was Abdul-Muttalib

Abu Talib, Hamzah, and Al-Abbas were his uncles

Some of his cousins were Ali Ibn Abi Talib, Ja'far Ibn Abi Talib, Abdullah Ibn Abbas and others.

When Prophet Muhammad ﷺ was a young boy he lived in the desert of Makkah.

His family sent him there to learn pure Arabic and to enjoy the healthy air.

Haleemah As-Sa'diyyah took care of him in the desert. She was a kind and loving lady. She was like a mother to Prophet Muhammad ﷺ . She loved him very much and he loved her. Her family also was very nice to him.

Muhammad ﷺ was from the tribe of
Quraysh قُرَيْش .
People of his tribe lived in Makkah. They used to travel to other places to buy and sell things.

They used to go from Makkah to Yemen in the winter time...

... and from Makkah to Syria in the summer time.

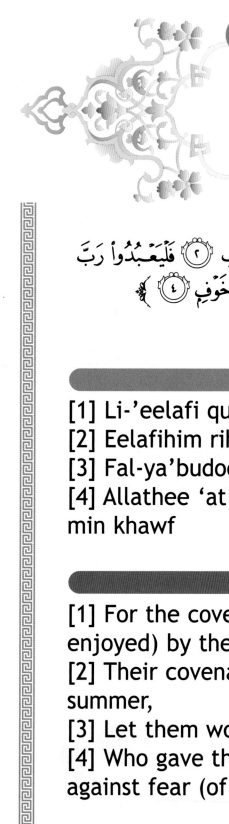
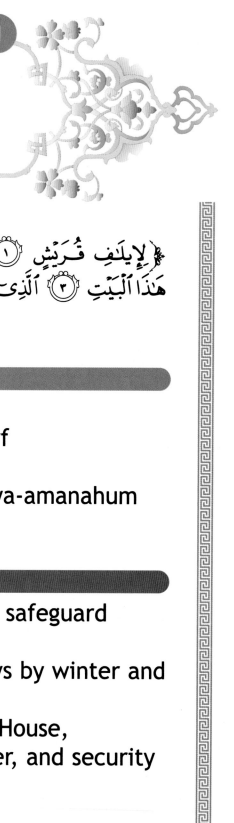

WORDS OF WISDOM
Holy Qur'an

سورة قريش
Surat Quraysh 106

بِّسْمِ لِإِيلَٰفِ قُرَيْشٍ ﴿١﴾ إِۦلَٰفِهِمْ رِحْلَةَ ٱلشِّتَآءِ وَٱلصَّيْفِ ﴿٢﴾ فَلْيَعْبُدُواْ رَبَّ هَٰذَا ٱلْبَيْتِ ﴿٣﴾ ٱلَّذِىٓ أَطْعَمَهُم مِّن جُوعٍ وَءَامَنَهُم مِّنْ خَوْفٍۭ ﴿٤﴾

TRANSLITERATION

[1] Li-'eelafi quraysh
[2] Eelafihim rihlat-ashshitaa'i-wassayf
[3] Fal-ya'budoo rabba hatha-lbayt
[4] Allathee 'at'amahum min joo'iw-wa-amanahum min khawf

TRANSLATION

[1] For the covenants (of security and safeguard enjoyed) by the Quraysh,
[2] Their covenants (covering) journeys by winter and summer,
[3] Let them worship the Lord of this House,
[4] Who gave them food against hunger, and security against fear (of danger).

Listen to the recitation of this sura, recite it and memorize it.

Prophet Muhammad's father had died before he was born. His mother died when he was still a very young boy. Prophet Muhammad was an orphan.

PROPHET MUHAMMAD WAS ALWAYS

Patient

when he was young, and also when he was old.

The Prophet's grandfather and uncles took great care of him. They loved him and kept him safe.

study questions

1 What city did the Prophet ﷺ live in when he was a child?

2 Who were his parents? What happened to them?

3 Who did the Prophet ﷺ live with in the desert?

4 What was the name of his tribe?

Muhammad Worked Hard

questions?

1 What was Muhammad's ﷺ first job?
2 How did Muhammad ﷺ treat animals?
3 How did Muhammad ﷺ treat other people?

word watch

As-Sadiq Al-Ameen   الصَّادِقُ الأمينْ
Shepherd   راعـي
Merchant   تاجِـر

When he was just a boy, Muhammad ﷺ was a **shepherd**. He took good care of sheep. He was kind with all animals.

Muhammad's ﷺ first job was a shepherd!!!

Muhammad's ﷺ second job was a merchant!!

When he was a young man, Muhammad ﷺ became a **merchant**. He traveled to places like Syria to buy, sell, and trade things.

Muhammad ﷺ was always kind and honest. People loved him very much, and they called him As-Sadiq Al-Ameen. This meant the Truth-teller and the Trustworthy.

He helped the poor and the needy people.

He solved problems between people and helped them stop fighting.

He was kind to everyone. He made people happy.

Everyone loved and trusted Muhammad ﷺ .

ACTIVITY time

Draw a sheep like the ones Prophet Muhammad ﷺ used to herd!

healthy habit

Always work hard to help your family and others as the Prophet ﷺ did.
Always be honest, tell the truth, and be kind with all people.

study questions

1. What was Prophet Muhammad's ﷺ first job?

2. What was his second job? What did he do?

3. How did Prophet Muhammad ﷺ help people?

4. Did people trust Muhammad ﷺ? What did they call him?

The Prophet's Family

questions?

1. Who was the Prophet's ﷺ first wife?
2. Did the Prophet ﷺ have children? How many?
3. How did the Prophet ﷺ treat his family?

word watch

Aalul-Bayt آل البَيْت
Khadeejah خَديجَة

When Prophet Muhammad ﷺ was a merchant, he worked for a great woman named **Khadeejah** رضي الله عنها. Prophet Muhammad ﷺ was a hard and honest worker. **Khadeejah** liked his good manners. Later, they got married.

Muhammad ﷺ had four daughters.

1. زَيْنَبْ
Zaynab

2. رُقَيَّة
Ruqayyah

3. أُمُّ كَلْثومْ
Ummu Kulthoom

4. فاطِمَةُ
Fatimah

He had three sons, but they died when they were young children.

1. القاسِمْ
Al-Qasim

2. عَبْدالله
Abdullah

3. إبْراهيمْ
Ibraheem

All of the Prophet's ﷺ children died while he was alive, except Fatimah. The Prophet ﷺ was sad, but patient.

Khadeejah رضي الله عنها was the mother of all the Prophet's children except Ibraheem. Ibraheem's mother was Mariyah رضي الله عنها .

After Khadeejah died, Prophet Muhammad ﷺ felt very sad. Later, he married other great women, like Sawdah, A'ishah, and Safiyyah.

The Prophet ﷺ had two grandsons: Al-Hasan and Al-Hussain. They were the children of Fatimah and her husband, Ali ibn Abi Talib, the cousin of Prophet Muhammad ﷺ.

We should love and respect the whole family of the Prophet. They are called "Aalul-Bayt"

The Prophet ﷺ loved his grandsons, and he played with them often. Muhammad ﷺ loved all children very much, and he took special care of them.

حديث شريف

Narrated By Ubn Majah & At-Tirmithi

عن عائشة رضي الله عنها: قال رسول الله ﷺ : "خَيرُكم خَيرُكُم لِأهْلِهِ وَأنا خَيرُكُمْ لِأهْلي"

رواه الترمذي وابن ماجه

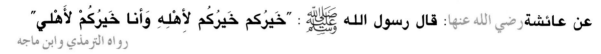

TRANSLITERATION

"Khayrukum Khayrukum Li-'ahlih, Wa-'ana Khayrukum Li Ahli."

TRANSLATION

"The best among you is the one who is best to his family, and I am the best of you to my family."

study questions

1 What was the name of Muhammad's ﷺ first wife?

2 How many sons did the Prophet ﷺ have? How many daughters did he have? How many children did he have all together?

3 What were the names of the Prophet's ﷺ children?

4 Which child of the Prophet lived the longest?

5 What were the names of the Prophet's grandchildren?

6 How did Muhammad ﷺ treat his grandsons and other children?

Muhammad Becomes a Prophet

questions?

1. When did Muhammad ﷺ become a Prophet?
2. Where did the Prophet receive the first ayaat of the Qur'an?
3. Who brought Al-Qur'an to Muhammad ﷺ from Allah?

word watch

Jabal-un-Noor	جَبَلُ النورْ
Ghar Hiraa'	غارُ حِراءْ
Jibreel	جِبْريلْ
Ayah	آيَـة
Ayaat	آياتْ
Nabiyy	نَبيّ
Rasool	رَسُول
Rasoolullah	رَسُولُ اللّه

■ Prophet Muhammad ﷺ used to go to a cave called Ghar Hiraa'. Ghar Hiraa' was in the top of a mountain called Jabal-un-Noor, or the Mountain of Light.

■ He used to stay in Ghar Hiraa' for several nights at a time. There he would think about the world and the One God who made it so beautiful.

One night, when Muhammad ﷺ was 40 years old, something strange and wonderful happened in Ghar Hiraa' during the month of Ramadan.

Muhammad ﷺ was visited by

ANGEL JIBREEL!!

Angel Jibreel is the leader of all angels. Allah has created angels out of light. They are kind, gentle, strong, and they have great faith. They obey Allah all the time. They do whatever Allah tells them to do. They love people. Angel Jibreel taught Prophet Muhammad ﷺ Al-Qur'an. He always told Muhammad ﷺ what Allah wanted him to do.

Angel Jibreel said to Muhammad ﷺ, "READ."

Muhammad ﷺ did not know how to read, and he said, "I can't read!"
Angel Jibreel repeated, "READ!"
Muhammad ﷺ again said, "I can't read!"
Then Angel Jibreel recited the first ayaat (verses) Prophet Muhammad ﷺ heard of Al-Qur'an. These were the first five ayaat of Surat-ul-'Alaq.

Muhammad now became a nabiyy, or Prophet.
Allah chose him to teach people the religion of Islam.
Rasool is another word for prophet. It means messenger.
Rasoolullah means "messenger of Allah." Muhammad ﷺ taught people the message, or book of Allah.

Muhammad ﷺ was very scared in the cave. He was alone in the cave, and it was dark.
This was the first time that he had seen an angel!

Muhammad ﷺ ran home to tell Khadeejah رضي الله عنها what had happened. Khadeejah made him feel better. She told him that Allah would take care of him because he was such a patient and nice person.

سورة العلق
Surat-ul-Alaq - 96

TRANSLITERATION

[1] Iqra' bismi rabbik-allathee khalaq
[2] Khalaq-al-insana min alaq
[3] Iqra' warabbuk-al-akram
[4] Allathee allama bilqalam
[5] Allam-al-insana ma lam ya'lam

TRANSLATION

[1] Recite! (or read!) in the name of your Lord, Who created-
[2] Created man, out of a clot of blood:
[3] Recite! And your Lord is the Most Generous,
[4] He taught (the use of) the pen,
[5] Taught man what he knew not.

Listen to the recitation of this sura, recite it and memorize it.

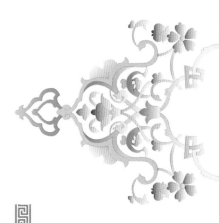

WORDS OF WISDOM
(Hadeeth Shareef)

حديث شريف

Narrated By Al-Bukhari

عن عثمان بن عفان رضي اللّه عنه: أن رسول اللّه ﷺ قال:
"خَيرُكُمْ مَنْ تَعَلَّمَ القُرْآنَ وَعَلَّمَهُ."
رواه البخاري

TRANSLITERATION

"Khayrukum man ta'allam-al-Qur'ana wa allamah."

TRANSLATION

Othman Ibn Affan reported that the Prophet ﷺ said: "The best among you is the one who learns the Qur'an and teaches it to others."

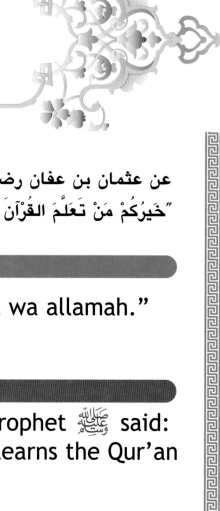

healthy
habit

Learn to read the Qur'an and memorize it every day.

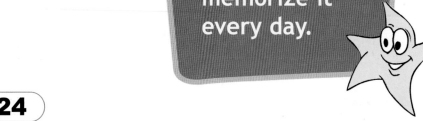

ACTIVITY time

Create a poster that has pictures of Makkah, Jabal-un-Noor, and Qur'an.

Listen to this nasheed about Prophet Muhammad and try to memorize it.

study

questions

1 Where did Muhammad ﷺ go to think about the world?

2 Who was Jibreel?

3 What was the first word Jibreel said to Muhammad ﷺ ?

4 Where did Muhammad ﷺ go after he met Jibreel?

5 What did Khadeejah say to make Muhammad ﷺ feel better?

6 Why do you think Muslims gave Jabal-un-noor this name?

7 Why do you think the first word of the Qur'an was "read?"

Sahabah, Friends of the Prophet

questions?

1 Who were the friends of the Prophet ﷺ ?
2 Why do you think they loved Rasoolullah ﷺ ?
3 What does the word Sahabah mean?
4 What did they do for him?

word watch

Sahabah	صَحابَة
Sahabi	صَحابِي
Sahabiyyat	صَحابِيَّاتْ
Abu-Bakr As-Siddeeq	أَبو بَكْرُ الصِّديق
'Omar Ibn Al-Khattab	عُمَرْ بِنْ الخَطّابْ
'Othman Ibn 'Affan	عُثْمانْ بِنْ عَفَّانْ
'Ali Ibn Abi-Talib	عَلي بِنْ أَبي طالِبْ

The Prophet ﷺ had many friends.

His BEST friend was:

أَبو بَكْرُ الصِّديق
'Abu-Bakr
As-Siddeeq

The Prophet's friends, or companions, are known as the Sahabah. **Sahabah** صَحابة is plural for **Sahabi** صَحابي .
A Sahabi is a friend of Prophet Muhammad ﷺ .

Some of his other friends were:

عُمَرْ بِنْ الخَطّابْ
'Omar
Ibn-ul-Khattab

رضي الله عنه

عُثمانْ بِنْ عَفّانْ
'Othman
Ibn Affan

رضي الله عنه

عَلي بِنْ أبي طالِبْ
'Ali
Ibn Abi Talib

رضي الله عنه

Other friends of the Prophet:

- Zaid Ibn Harithah زيد بن حارثة رضي الله عنه was very special to the Prophet ﷺ.
- Bilal Ibn Rabah بلال بن رباح رضي الله عنه gave the first athan, and he was the Mu'athin.
- Khalid Ibn-ul-Waleed خالد بن الوليد رضي الله عنه was a great leader of the Muslim army.
- Osama Ibn Zaid أسامة بن زيد رضي الله عنه was the youngest Muslim general, he was 17 years old.
- Mus'ab Ibn Omair مصعب بن عمير رضي الله عنه was a great young teacher of Islam.
- Ja'far Ibn Abi-Talib جعفر بن أبي طالب رضي الله عنه was the Prophet's cousin.

They helped the Prophet ﷺ teach Islam to people all the time. They helped him in Makkah. They helped him in Madinah.

THE SAHABAH ARE MY HEROES!

The women companions of the Prophet ﷺ are called Sahabiyyat.

Some of his Sahabiyyat were:

خَـوْلَـة

Khawlah

Bint-ul-Azwar

نُـسَـيْـبَـة

Nusaybah

Bint Ka'b

(Ummu Amarah)

أَسْـمـاءْ

Asmaa'

Bint Abu Bakr

رضي الله عنها

رضي الله عنها

رضي الله عنها

All the Sahabah and Sahabiyyat LOVED the Prophet ﷺ very much.

healthy

habit

We should love all the Sahabah and Sahabiyyat. Whenever you say the name of a Sahabi, say:

رَضِيَ اللّه عنْـه   "Radiy-Allah Anhu."

If she is a woman you say:

رَضِيَ اللّه عنْـها   "Radiy-Allah Anha."

This means: "May Allah be pleased with him or her"

Allah loved As-Sahabah because they were excellent Muslims. Allah said that He is pleased with them and promised them Jannah.

study

questions

1 What do we call the friends of the Prophet ﷺ?

2 What were some of the names of the Sahabah?

3 Who was Muhammad's ﷺ best friend?

4 Where did the Sahabah help the Prophet ﷺ?

5 What did Allah say about the Sahabah?

6 What can we do to follow the example of the Sahabah?

WORSHIPPING ALLAH

Arkan-ul-Islam, The Five Pillars of Islam

questions?

1 What are somethings that ALL Muslims must do?
2 How many pillars of Islam do you know?
3 How many pillars of Islam do you practice?

word watch

Arkan-ul-Islam	أَرْكانُ الإِسْلامْ
Shahadah	شَهادَة
Salah	صَلاة
Al-Ka'bah	الكَعْبَة
Sawm	صَوْمْ
Siyam	صِيامْ
Ramadan	رَمَضان
Zakah	زَكاة
Hajj	حَجّ

Muslims come from many places, but they practice the same acts of worship.

All Muslims believe in the five pillars of Islam, Arkan-ul-Islam.

Arkan-ul-Islam

1 The first pillar is the Shahadah.

The **Shahadah** is the Muslim statement of faith. It is said in Arabic:

أشهد أن لا إله إلا الله وأشهد أن محمدا رسول الله.

"Ash'hado an la ilaha illAllah wa ash'hado anna Muhammadan ﷺ rasoolullah."

This means that you believe in only one God, Allah. It means also that Muhammad ﷺ is the messenger of Allah. We say the Shahadah in every prayer and in our dua'a.

Allah alone created us, and He created Rasoolullah to be our role model. He taught us what is right and wrong.

healthy h a b i t

Say the Shahadah as many times as you can. You will get many hasanat every time you say it.
This means that we believe in only One God, Allah, and that Muhammad is the messenger of Allah.

C3

2 The second pillar is Salah.

Salah means prayer. Muslims pray to Allah five times a day. No matter where we are, we pray to Allah. We face the direction of **Al-Ka'bah** in Makkah. Prayer is a way for us to show Allah that we love Him. During Salah we thank Him for all His gifts. Allah says:

﴿ وَأَقِيمُواْ ٱلصَّلَوٰةَ ﴾ البقرة: ٤٣

Wa Aqeemos –Salah
(And offer prayer)

healthy
h a b i t

Learn how to do Salah, and always pray on time.

3 The third pillar is Sawm or Siyam.

Muslims fast during the days of the month of **Ramadan**. We fast by not eating or drinking from dawn until sunset. We also try to be on our best behavior. Fasting can make you hungry. This lets you feel how poor people feel every day.

Fasting teaches you to control yourself by not eating or drinking when you are hungry or thirsty.

﴿ يَـٰٓأَيُّهَا ٱلَّذِينَ ءَامَنُوا۟ كُتِبَ عَلَيْكُمُ ٱلصِّيَامُ كَمَا كُتِبَ عَلَى ٱلَّذِينَ مِن قَبْلِكُمْ لَعَلَّكُمْ تَتَّقُونَ ﴿١٨٣﴾ ﴾ البقرة: ١٨٣

"Ya ayyuha-llatheena amanoo kutiba alaykum-us-siyamu kama kutiba ala-llatheena min qablikum la'allakum tattaqoon."

Oh you who believe! Fasting is prescribed to you as it was prescribed to those before you, that you may be mindful of God.

Al-Baqarah - Ayah 183

healthy
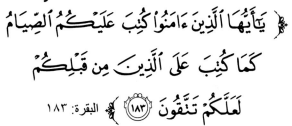
habit

Learn how to fast, and try to fast the whole month of Ramadan.

The fourth pillar is Zakah.

Zakah is charity money that we give to help the poor. Muslims should always help out others when they can. One way to help the poor is by giving them money.

Allah says:

﴾ وَءَاتُواْ ٱلزَّكَوٰةَ ﴿ البقرة: ٤٣

Wa Atoz -Zakah

(And give Zakah)

healthy
h a b i t

Give charity to the poor when you have extra money. If you do not have money, smile at people. Prophet Muhammad taught us that smiling is charity too.

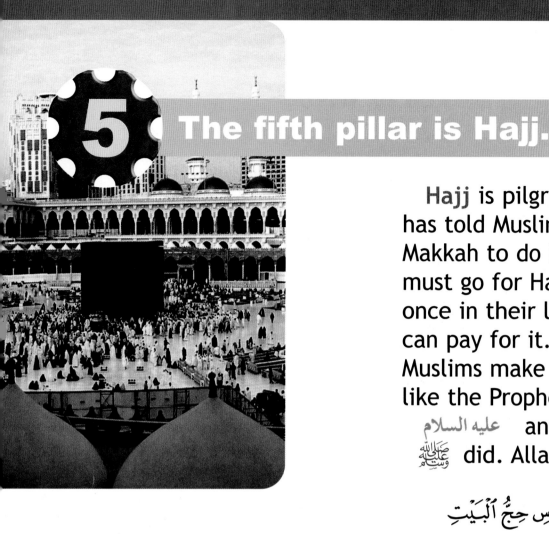

Hajj is pilgrimage. Allah has told Muslims to go to Makkah to do Hajj. Muslims must go for Hajj at least once in their lifetime if they can pay for it. In Makkah, Muslims make a pilgrimage like the Prophets Ibraheem عليه السلام and Muhammad ﷺ did. Allah Says:

﴿ وَلِلَّهِ عَلَى ٱلنَّاسِ حِجُّ ٱلْبَيْتِ مَنِ ٱسْتَطَاعَ إِلَيْهِ سَبِيلًا ﴾ آل عمران: ٩٧

"Wa lillahi Alan-Nasi Hijj-ul-bayti man istataa'a Ilayhi Sabeela."

(Hajj to the house [of Allah in Makkah] is a duty for Allah on all people who can make the trip.)

Al-'Imran - Ayah 97

healthy

h a b i t

At the time of Hajj, watch a movie or read a book about Hajj, and have your parents explain Hajj to you.

WORDS OF WISDOM
Hadeeth Shareef

حديث شريف

Narrated by Muslim & Bukhari

عن ابن عمر رضي اللّه عنه: قال رسول اللّه ﷺ :

بُنِي الإسلام على خمس: شهادةٍ أن لا إله إلا اللّه وأن محمداً رسول اللّه وإقام الصَّلاةِ وإيتاءِ الزكاةِ وصومِ رمضانَ وحجِّ البيت"

رواه البخاري ومسلم

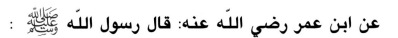

TRANSLITERATION

"Boniya-Al-Islamu ala Khams, Shahadati an la ilaha illa-Allah wa anna Muhammadan Rasoolullah wa Iqami-Salah, wa ita'i-Zakah, wa sawmu Ramadan wa Hajj-ul-Bayt."

TRANSLATION

Ibn Omar رضي الله عنه reported that the Prophet ﷺ said: "Islam is built on five pillars; to witness that there is no God but Allah, and Muhammad is the messenger of Allah, to do the prayers, to give charity, to fast Ramadan, and to go to Hajj (if you can go there)."

ACTIVITY time

Draw a masjid that has five pillars, and write the name of one pillar of Islam on each pillar of the masjid you draw.

PILLARS OF ISLAM

Listen to a nasheed about the Pillars of Islam and try to memorize it.

study

questions

1. Can you count how many times a day you say the Shahadah during Salah?

2. Where do you face when you pray? And how many times should a Muslim pray every day?

3. In what month do Muslims practice the fourth pillar (Sawm)?

4. Who does Zakah help?

5. How many times must a Muslim make Hajj? Where do Muslims go for Hajj?

I Love Salah, Prayer

questions?

1. What is the key to Jannah?
2. How can we be with Rasoolullah ﷺ in Jannah?
3. What are the names of the five daily prayers?

word watch

Fajr	فَجْرْ
Thuhr	ظُهْرْ
Asr	عَصْرْ
Maghrib	مَغْرِبْ
Isha'	عِشَاءْ

Zaid saw his father praying one day. When his father finished, Zaid asked him:

Zaid: Baba, why do we pray?

Baba: Allah ﷻ created us to worship Him. When we pray, we worship Him and show our love for Him ﷻ.

When we love Allah ﷻ, Allah loves us even more. He gives us happiness in this life, and Jannah in the life after.

Also, when we pray, we thank Allah ﷻ for everything He has given us.

Zaid: Wow, doing our salah brings us so many good things! I used to think that it was hard to pray so many times, but now I know that Allah has told us to pray because it is GOOD for us!

Baba: Yes, Zaid. keeping up with your prayers will take you somewhere special. *Listen to this story:*

Story Time

Once a young Sahabi (a friend of the Prophet ﷺ) named Rabi'ah bin Ka'b, asked to be with the Prophet in Jannah. Rabi'ah was 14 years old. The Prophet ﷺ asked him:

"Is there anything else you want Rabi'ah?" Rabi'ah answered "No. All I want is to be with you in Jannah." The Prophet ﷺ said: ''أَعِنِّي عَلَى نَفْسِكَ بِكَثْرَةِ السُّجُودِ''

"Then help yourself by making plenty of Salah"
Narrated by Muslim

Zaid: So Salah will even help us be with Rasoolullah ﷺ in Jannah!

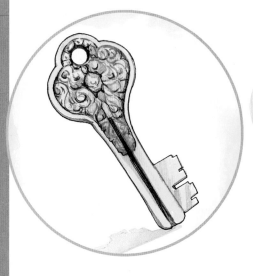

Do you know what the key to Jannah is?

Prayer is the key to Paradise!!

Baba asked Zaid: Now, do you know what the five daily prayers are?

Zaid: Let me think...Fajr, Thuhr, Asr, Maghrib, and Isha'!

Baba: Very good! Now do you know what times we do these prayers?

Zaid: I think I need some help here.

Baba smiled: Of course. Let's go through them together.

FAJR

We pray Fajr before the sun rises in the morning.

THUHR

We pray Thuhr in the early afternoon, after lunchtime.

ASR

We pray Asr in the late afternoon, when the sun is a little low in the sky.

MAGHRIB

We pray Maghrib right after the sun sets.

ISHA'

We pray 'Isha' at night, before we go to sleep.

WORDS OF WISDOM
(Hadeeth Shareef)

حديث شريف

Narrated By Muslim & Bukhari

عن عبدالله بن مسعود رضي الله عنه قال: سألت النبي ﷺ :
أي العمل أحب إلى الله؟ قال: الصلاة على وقتها."

رواه البخاري ومسلم

TRANSLITERATION

Abdullah Ibn Mas'ood (R): Ayyul 'Amali Ahabbu IlAllah?
The Prophet ﷺ said: "As-Salatu Ala Waqtiha."

TRANSLATION

Abdullah Ibn Mas'ood asked the Prophet ﷺ what is the good deed that Allah loves the most? The Prophet ﷺ answered: Praying right on time.

Follow the Prophet's way,

pray 5 times a day!

ACTIVITY time

Make a chart like this to help you keep track of your prayers:

Prayer	MON	TUES	WED	THURS	FRI	SAT	SUN
Fajr	✔	✔					
Thuhr	✔	✔					
Asr	✔	✔					
Maghrib	✔						
Isha	✔						

"SALAH"
Listen to a nasheed about Salah and try to memorize it.

study

questions

1 Why do we pray to Allah? Give three reasons.

2 What can you do to be with the Prophet ﷺ in Jannah?

3 What is the first prayer of the day? What is the last prayer?

4 What is the prayer right after sunset?

5 Can you draw a Muslim praying?

Wudoo' Makes Me Clean

questions?

1. What should we do before doing prayers?
2. What body parts do we clean when we make wudoo'?
3. What should you say before and after you make wudoo'?
4. Can wudoo' be broken? What breaks your wudoo'?

word watch

Niyyah	نِيَة
Wudoo'	وُضـوْء
Taharah	طَهارَة

WORDS OF WISDOM

Holy Qur'an

سورة المائدة

Surat-ul-Ma'ida: Ayah 6

﴿ يَـٰٓأَيُّهَا ٱلَّذِينَ ءَامَنُوٓاْ إِذَا قُمۡتُمۡ إِلَى ٱلصَّلَوٰةِ فَٱغۡسِلُواْ وُجُوهَكُمۡ وَأَيۡدِيَكُمۡ إِلَى ٱلۡمَرَافِقِ وَٱمۡسَحُواْ بِرُءُوسِكُمۡ وَأَرۡجُلَكُمۡ إِلَى ٱلۡكَعۡبَيۡنِ ﴾ المائدة: ٦

FULL TRANSLITERATION

"Ya ayyuha-allatheena amanoo itha qumtum ila-assalati faighsiloo wujoohakum wa-aydiyakum ila-almarafiqi wamsahoo biru'oosikum wa-arjulakum ila-alka'bayn."

TRANSLATION

"Oh you who believe! when you prepare for prayer, wash your faces, and your hands (and arms) to the elbows; wipe your heads (with water); and (wash) your feet to the ankles."

Listen to the recitation of this sura, recite it and memorize it.

Allah told us to be in a state of Taharah before Salah. Taharah (cleanliness) means to be in a state of purity. Our Salah won't count if we have not cleaned certain parts of our body. The action of cleaning these parts is called wudoo'. So we must make wudoo' whenever we pray. Let's go through wudoo' step-by-step!

healthy
habit

When you enter the bathroom, say your dua'a:

اللَّهمَ إنِّي أَعوذُ بِك مِنَ الخُبْثِ والخَبائثْ

"Allahumma inni a'oothu bika minal kubuthi wal kabaa'ith"

It means: "Oh Allah protect me from dirt and devils."
Remember to step in with your LEFT foot first!
When you are done, step out with your right foot!

This is how Dad taught me to make wudoo':

1 I make my niyyah. I say in my mind what I am about to do. Here, my niyyah is to make wudoo'.

2 I say "Bismillah," which means "in the name of Allah." This reminds us that we are making wudoo' for Allah.

3 Then, I wash my hands THREE times up to my wrists. This reminds me to do only good things with my hands.

4 After that, I rinse out my mouth THREE times using my right hand. I use my mouth to eat and talk. So, I should eat only good things and say only nice words.

5 Then, I rinse the inside of my nose and blow it using my left hand THREE times. This reminds me to be thankful to Allah for giving me a sense of smell.

6 After that, I wash my face THREE times. I make sure water cleans my face from the hair on my forehead down to my chin, and from my right ear to the left ear.

7 Then, I wash my arms all the way up to my elbows THREE times. I wash my right arm before my left arm. The Prophet ﷺ told us to do good things with our right hands.

8 Then, I wet my hands a little, and wipe my head from the front to the back. Then I bring my hands back to the front again. I do this once.

9 Then, I gently wipe the inside and the back of my ears with some more water. This teach me to listen only to good things.

10 Now I am ready to wash my feet. I wash both feet up to my ankles THREE times. I wash my RIGHT foot FIRST. I make sure the water gets between my toes and clean any dirt that may be there. Cleaning my feet helps me remember to go to good places.

Now we are done making wudoo'! Allahu Akbar! Now that I am done making wudoo', I say the sha-hadah.

"أَشْـهَدُ أَنْ لا إِله إِلاَّ اللّه وَأَشْـهَدُ أَنَّ مُـحَمّداً رَسُولُ اللّه"

Ash-hadu an La Ilaha Ill-Allah, Wa Ash-hadu anna Muhammadan Rasoolullah!

WORDS OF WISDOM
(Hadeeth Shareef)

حديث شريف

Narrated By Ahmad & At-Tirmithi

عن ابن عامر رضي الله عنه: أن رسول الله ﷺ قال:
"من توضأ فأحسن الوضوء فقال أشهد أن لا إله إلا الله وحده لا شريك له وأن محمدا عبده ورسوله فتحت له ثمانية أبواب من الجنة يدخل من أيها شاء."

رواه الترمذي وأحمد

TRANSLITERATION

"Man Tawadda'a fa-ahsan-alwudoo'a faqala ash-hadu an la ilaha ill-Allah wahdahu la shareeka lahu wa anna Muhammadan Abduhu wa rasooluhu futihat lahu thamaniyatu abwabin min al-Jannah yadkhulu min ayyuha shaa'."

TRANSLATION

"He who performs wudoo' perfectly, and then recites the Shahadah, the eight gates of Jannah would open for him [on the day of judgment] to enter through any one he wishes."

healthy
h a b i t

Always have your Wudoo', so you will be ready to pray all the time!

Things that Break Your Wudoo'

You must remember that some things can break your wudoo'! If you:

- ■ use the restroom
- ■ pass gas
- ■ fall asleep

you must make wudoo' **again** before you pray.

healthy
habit

1. When you are in the bathroom, remember that you should:
   - keep yourself clean
   - Keep the bathroom clean
2. Try not to talk when you are in the bathroom.
3. When you leave the bathroom, step out with your RIGHT foot and say:

"Ghufraanak"   "غُـفْـرانَك"

It means: [Oh Allah I want] your forgiveness

ACTIVITY time

Find a partner and practice making wudoo' with him/her. Remind each other of the order everything is washed, and how many times it is washed.

" WUDOO' "

Listen to this nasheed and try to memorize it.

study

questions

1 List parts of your body that are washed in wudoo'.

2 What parts are washed only ONCE?

3 What do you say before and after you make your wudoo'?

4 What side do you start each step with? Why?

5 What things can break your wudoo'?

6 What dua'a do you say when entering and leaving the restroom?

Zaid Learns How to Pray

questions?

1. What are the different movements in Salah?
2. Where do we face when we pray?
3. Does every prayer have the same number of Rak'aat?

word watch

Qiyam	قِيامْ
Rukoo'	رُكوعْ
Sujood	سُجودْ
Juloos	جُلوسْ
Tasleem	تَسْليمْ
Rak'ah	رَكْعَة
Rak'aat	رَكَعات
Qiblah	قِبْلَة
Fard	فَرْضْ
Tashahhud	تَشَهُّدْ
Assalatul Ibraheemiyyah	الصَلاةُ الإِبراهيمِيَة
Hasanat	حسنات

Zaid knew his birthday was coming up. He was going to turn seven! But there was something more important than turning seven. Zaid was going to learn how to pray! Zaid ran to Dad.

Zaid asked: "Dad, can you teach me how to make Salah?"
Dad said: " Of course, Zaid. Lets learn Salah together!
Remember, first you have to make wudoo'!"

Zaid made wudoo', and Dad began to teach Zaid how to pray.

Salat-ul-Fajr

1 You face the **Qiblah** and make Niyyah (intention) in your heart. Niyyah is knowing what you are about to do and why you are doing it. You should always make sure you pray and do all good deeds for Allah.

What is the Qiblah, Dad?

The Qiblah is the place you face when you pray. It is toward Al-Ka'bah, in Makkah.

2 You raise your hands behind your ears and say

اللّٰهُ أَكْـبَـرْ

"Allahu Akbar" (Allah is Greater).

3 While you are standing, you put your right hand over your left hand by your belly bottom. This is called Qiyam. You read Surat-ul-Fatihah and a short Surah or few Ayat.

4 You say الله أكبر , "Allahu Akbar," then make Rukoo'. Rukoo' is when you bow down and put both hands on your knees.

5 During Rukoo' you say
سُبحانَ ربي العظيم
"Subhana Rabiyal Atheem"
(Glory to my Lord the Great)
THREE times.

6 You rise from Rukoo' and say
سَمِعَ اللّه لِمنْ حَمِدَه، ربنا ولك الحمد
"Sami'a-Allahu Liman Hamidah"
(Allah hears those who praise Him).
Then, you say "Rabbana Wa Lak-Al-Hamd" (Our Lord, we praise you).

7 You say اللّهُ أُكْـبَـرْ , then make Sujood by resting your forehead, nose, hands, knees and toes on the floor. You say سُبْحان رَبِّي الأعلى , "Subhana Rabiyal A'la" (Glory be to Allah, the Most High) THREE times.

8 You sit up from Sujood while saying اللّهُ أُكْـبَـرْ . Then repeat Sujood again.

You just completed one full **Rak'ah**!! A Rak'ah is made up of **Qiyam**, 1 **Rukoo'**, and 2 **Sujood**!

9 To start the second Rak'ah, you stand up saying اللّهُ أُكْـبَـرْ , from sujood, and repeat steps 3 to 8 .

10 After you finish the second Rak'ah, you sit down (Juloos) to read At-Tashahhud and As-Salatul Ibraheemiyyah.

ACTIVITY time

Practice two Rak'aat with your classmates.

التشهُّد
At-Tashahhud

التحيات لله والصلوات والطيبات،
السلام عليك أيها النبي ورحمة الله وبركاته،
السلام علينا وعلى عباد الله الصالحين،
أشهد أن لا إله إلا الله وحده لا شريك له،
وأشهد أن محمدا عبده ورسوله.

At-Tahayyatu lillahi wassalawatu wattayyibat,
Assalamu 'alayka 'ayyuhan-nabiyyu warahmat-ullahi wabarakatuh,
Assalamu 'alayna wa 'ala ibad-illahis-saliheen,
Ashahadu 'alla 'ilaha illAllah wahdahu la shari-ca lah
wa 'ash-hadu anna Muhammadan 'abduhu wa rasooluh

الصَّلاة الإبراهيمية
As-Salatul Ibraheemiyyah

اللهم صلٍّ على محمد وعلى آل محمد
كما صليت على إبراهيم وعلى آل إبراهيم
وبارك على محمد وعلى آل محمد
كما باركت على إبراهيم وعلى آل إبراهيم
في العالمين، إنك حميد مجيد.

Allahumma salli 'ala Muhammad wa 'ala aali Muhammad
Kama sallayta 'ala Ibraheem wa 'ala aali Ibraheem
wa barek 'ala Muhammad wa 'ala aali Muhammad
Kama barakta 'ala Ibraheem wa 'ala aali Ibraheem
Fi-l'aalameen, innaka hameedun majeed

Memorize this important portion of the five daily prayers.

11 You turn your face to the right side and say:
" السلام عليكم ورحمة الله "
"Assalamu Alaykum wa Rahmatu-Llah" (Peace and Mercy of Allah be upon you).

12 You turn your face to the left side and say the same.
This is called Tasleem.

Zaid was so happy to learn how to make Salah!!!

Zaid had another question.

Zaid: Dad, I know that we have to do 5 Fard (required) prayers every day; Fajr, Thuhr, 'Asr, Maghrib, and 'Isha. Are the rak'aat the same for all the prayers?

Dad: Excellent question, Zaid. The number of Rak'aat for some of these Fard prayers is not the same. They can have 2 or 3 or 4 Rak'aat.

Zaid: I know how to pray 2 rak'aat, because you just taught me that. But how about 3 and 4 rak'aat?

Dad: Well, for Maghrib, you have three rak'aat. The first 2 rak'aat are like Fajr salat, except you go back into Qiyaam after your Tashahhud. The last Rak'ah will be normal, but you don't read a short surah after Al-Fatihah. Then in Juloos, you say your Tashahhud and Assalatul Ibraheemiyyah, and end with tasleem.

Let's remember this:

- **Fajr**   2 rak'aat
- Thuhr   4 rak'aat
- **'Asr**   4 rak'aat
- Maghrib   3 rak'aat
- **'Isha**   4 rak'aat

Zaid: How about 4 rak'aat?

Dad: For 4 **rak'aat** prayers, you do your first two rak'aat like Fajr, but you get up after the tashahhud. You repeat the same steps for the next 2 rak'aat. You just need to remember that you don't read a short surah after **Al-Fatihah** in the third and forth rak'aat.

Zaid: How am I going to remember all this, Dad?!

Dad: The more you practice, the easier it will get. Don't worry, son, I will help you. I know you can do it, insha Allah!

In a few days, Zaid said to Dad:

Zaid: Dad, Salah is so much easier now! The more I pray to Allah, the more I love it!

Dad: I knew you would do a great job in your salah, Zaid. I am very proud of you. Today, I bought you a present, it is a prayer rug.

Zaid: Oh, Jazakallahu Khayran dad, I love you.

Zaid enjoyed every Salah he made after that. He thanked his father for teaching him and for the great present. He also knew Allah would give him **Hasanat**, or good deeds.

ACTIVITY time

Practice a 3 rak'aat prayer and a 4 rak'aat prayer with your classmates. Have your teacher or parent watch you.

healthy habit

Always pray your Salah on time!!

study

questions

1 What movements is one Rak'ah made of?

2 Where is the Qiblah?

3 What should you say in your heart before you pray?

4 How many Rak'aat are in Fajr prayer? How about Thuhr, 'Asr, Maghrib and 'Isha?

5 Draw a picture of a Muslim child doing Qiyam, Rukoo', Sujood, and Juloos.

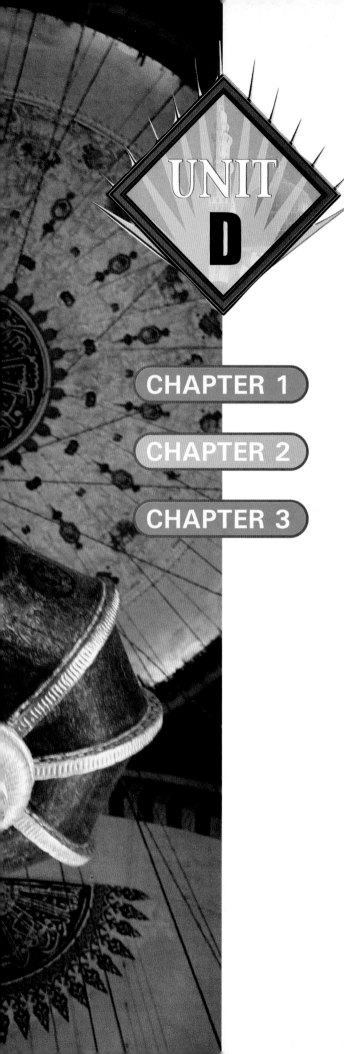

UNIT D

MY MUSLIM WORLD

My Muslim Brothers and Sisters

questions?

1. What country do you live in? What city?
2. Do you have friends or family in other cities? How about in other countries?
3. What are three places in the world that are special to all Muslims?

word watch

Ummah	أُمَّـة
Akh	أَخْ
Ukht	أُخْـتْ

MUSLIMS come in all different colors and looks.

Muslims are all brothers and sisters in Islam.
We are all one **Ummah**. An **Ummah** is the community of Muslims.

Allah made the world for us
to live together
in love and peace.

Muslims live ALL OVER THE WORLD!!!
We are all brothers and sisters in Islam!!!

Muslims share many things

All Muslims believe in one God, Allah ﷻ . They follow the same prophet, Muhammad ﷺ

All Muslims pray toward one qiblah, Al-Ka'bah, in Makkah. Muslims go to Makkah for Hajj, all wearing the same thing.

Allah loves it when Muslims pray in Jama'ah. All Muslims are equal in front of God. The best among them is the more pious. They are only different to Him by their level of faith and good deeds.

All Muslims love the three holy cities: Makkah, Madinah, and Al-Quds (Jerusalem). Allah made very interesting things happen at these three places a long time ago. That is why they are special. We will learn all about these cities later.

Did you know that there are more than 1 BILLION and a half Muslims in the world?

أَخ (Akh) in Arabic means "brother"

Wow! I have more than a billion brothers and sisters in Islam! That is great. I don't even think I can count that high!

أُخْت (Ukht) in Arabic means "Sister"

There are over 55 Muslim countries.

Egypt

Indonesia

Somalia

Pakistan

Muslims live in all countries around the world.

Muslims Live In Spain and France

Muslims Live In India

Muslims Live In China

Muslims Live In The United States

There are **seven million Muslims** in the United States.

There are around **2000 mosques** in America.

A mosque in Tempe, Arizona, USA.

All the Muslims in the world make up

the **Muslim Ummah**

We  all our brothers and sisters around the world.

WORDS OF WISDOM

Holy Qur'an & Hadeeth Shareef

قرآن كريم
وحديث شريف

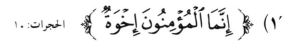

١) ﴿ إِنَّمَا ٱلْمُؤْمِنُونَ إِخْوَةٌ ﴾ الحجرات: ١٠

٢) "المسلم أخو المسلم" رواه البخاري ومسلم عن عبدالله بن عمر رضي الله عنه

TRANSLITERATION

1. "Innamal-Mu'minoona Ikhwah"

2. "Al-Muslimu Akh-ul-Muslim"

TRANSLATION

1. "Believers are Brothers." 49:10
2. "The Muslim is a brother to another Muslim."

A Hadeeth reported by Abdullah Ibn Umar in Al-Bukhari and Muslim

ACTIVITY time

Collect pictures of 10 mosques from different countries around the world.
Stick them on a poster board.

study

questions

1 Do Muslims come from Japan? How about Canada? Mexico? Russia? Germany?

2 Name some Muslim countries.

3 How many Muslims live in the world?

4 What are some things that all Muslims share?

5 What do we call the Muslim community in the world?

6 How would you say "brother" and "sister" in Arabic?

Assalamu Alaykum Peace on You

questions?

1. How should you greet another Muslim?
2. Why do Muslims say Assalamu Alaykum? And what does it mean?
3. When do Muslims say Assalamu Alaykum?

word watch

Assalamu Alaykum السَّلام عَليكُم
Wa-Alaykum Assalam وعَليكُم السَّلام

Assalamu Alaykum!

That means "Peace be Upon You!"
We say this whenever we meet a
Muslim and when we leave a Muslim!

السَّلامُ عَلَيْكُم

This is the Muslim greeting.

We say

السَّلام عليكُم

"Assalamu Alaykum"

to our family when we wake up in the morning and when we go to sleep at night.

We say

السَّلام عليكُم

"Assalamu Alaykum"

when we see our friends and teachers at school, and when we leave them to go home.

We say

السَّلام عليكُم

"Assalamu Alaykum"

when we meet Muslims at a store.

We say

السَّلام عليكُم

"Assalamu Alaykum"

to our brothers and sisters at the masjid before and after prayers.

We say

السَّلام عليكُم

"Assalamu Alaykum"

to our family when we come home.

AND THEY ALL SAY:

وعليكُم السَّلام

"WA-ALAYKUM ASSALAM!"

That means "Peace be Upon You, Too!"
It gives us so many good deeds!

Allah (is) As-Salam

السَّلامُ

The Source of Peace

Allah gives peace to the world. We should always wish peace upon the people around us by saying "Assalamu Alaykum."

Muslims all over the world say

السَّلامُ عَليكُم   *"Assalamu Alaykum!"*

People say "hello," "hi," "hey," and "what's up" when they meet. They also say "bye" when they leave each other. It is better for Muslims to say "Assalamu Alaykum." This has a very good meaning and gives Muslims many hasanat every day. It also makes Muslims love each other more.

healthy

 **habit**

Always say السَّلام عليكُم
"Assalamu Alaykum" when you see another Muslim. Never forget to say "Walaykum Assalam" if someone says "Assalamu Alaykum" to you first.

ACTIVITY time

Count how many times you say "Assalamu Alaykum" today. Every time you give salam to someone, put a smiley face on an index card. The more you say it to others, the more hasanat you get.

study

questions

1 What does "Assalamu Alaykum" mean?

2 Which is better, to say "Hi" or "Assalamu Alaykum" when you meet or leave other Muslims? Why?

3 If someone says "Assalamu Alaykum" to you, how should you reply?

4 Name some places where you meet Muslims.

5 How can you get more hasanat when you greet others?

Eid Mubarak

questions?

1 What holidays do you celebrate?
2 How many times a year do you have this holiday?
3 What do you do on this day?

word watch

Eid ul-Fitr	عيد الفِطْر
Eid ul-Adha	عيدُ الأضْحى
Ramadan	رمضان
Hajj	حج
Thul Hijjah	ذو الحجة
Takbeer	تكبير
Udhiyah	أُضْحِيَة
khutbah	خُطْبَة

Muslims

CELEBRATE EID

twice **a year.**

Muslims all over the world celebrate Eid together.

The FIRST Eid is عيد الفطر

Eid-ul-Fitr

Muslims celebrate **Eid-ul-Fitr** for three days after fasting the month of Ramadan. We know it is Eid when we see the new moon.

The SECOND Eid is عيد الأضحى

Eid-ul-Adha

Muslims celebrate Eid-ul-Adha in the month of **Thul-Hijjah** during the time of **Hajj**. The celebration lasts for four days. On this Eid, Muslims make **Udhiyah**, or sacrifice. They share the **Udhiyah** meat with friends, family, and the poor.

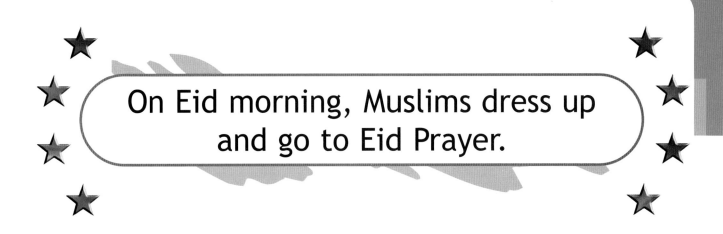

On Eid morning, Muslims dress up and go to Eid Prayer.

1. They say the Eid **Takbeer** together,

2. They pray two rak'aat of Salat-ul-Eid.

3. Then they listen to a special Eid **Khutbah**, or speech.

4. Then everyone hugs and says:

عيد مُبارَك

EID MUBARAK!!!

Takbeer of Eid

اللّه أَكْبَرْ، اللّه أَكْبَرْ، اللّه أَكْبَرْ، لا إلهَ إلاّ اللّه
اللّه أَكْبَرْ، اللّه أَكْبَرْ، ولِلّهِ الحَمْدُ

Allahu Akbar, Allahu Akbar , Allahu Akbar,
la ilaha illa-Allah

Allahu Akbar, Allahu Akbar , Wa lillahil-hamd

This means: Allah is greater, Allah is greater,
Allah is greater, There is no God but Allah

This means: Allah is greater, Allah is greater,
and praise be to Allah

Children receive gifts and money

Allah loves us. He gave us Eid so we can celebrate and be happy.

Families visit each other and eat yummy food

REMEMBER

There are Muslims in the world who don't get a wonderful Eid. Sometimes they don't have enough food to eat or money to buy Eid gifts. We should always be generous and give others as much as we can so all Muslims can have a beautiful Eid.

ACTIVITY time

1. Draw a picture of what you do on Eid.
2. Sit with your friends and say the takbeer of Eid together.

"EID MUBARAK"
Listen to a nasheed about Eid and try to memorize it.

study

questions

1 How many times a year do Muslims celebrate Eid?

2 What are the names of the two Eids?

3 How long is Eid-ul-Fitr?
What about Eid-ul-Adha?

4 What do Muslims do after the Eid prayer?

5 What special things do Muslims do on Eid-ul-Adha?

6 What is fun about Eid?

UNIT E

MY MUSLIM MANNERS

Allah Loves Kindness

questions?

1 Who should we treat kindly?
2 How can good deeds help us?
3 How should we treat animals and plants?
4 What would happen if we were mean to people, animals, and plants?

word watch

[Al-Lateef اللَّطِيفْ]

Did you know that even a small good deed can help you enter Jannah?

Also, a small bad deed can make Allah ﷻ unpleased with you!

Allah loves us very much, and wants us to love each other.

Allah is Kind, and He wants us to be kind to each other.

We should be kind to our parents. We should obey and respect them all the time.

We should be kind to relatives, friends, and neighbors. We should respect them and help them whenever they need help.

We should even be kind to animals and plants. We should not hurt animals, or destroy flowers and good plants.

There are many kinds of animals in the world. Allah ﷻ created them all. We use some animals for food, like chicken.

Some animals are for riding, like horses. Some animals make good pets, like cats. They can be fun to play with!

Allah (is) Al-Lateef

اللطيف

The Kind

WORDS OF WISDOM
(Hadeeth Shareef)

حديث شريف

Narrated by Muslim.

عن شداد بن أوس رضي الله عنه: قال رسول الله ﷺ :
"إن الله كتب الإحسان على كل شيء"

TRANSLITERATION

"Inna-Allaha katab-al-Ihsana ala kulli Shay'."

TRANSLATION

Shaddad Ibn Aws reported that the Prophet ﷺ said:
"Allah ordered that we be gentle with everything."

Allah ﷻ wants us to be
kind to His creations.

Let us read a story that Prophet Muhammad ﷺ told us:

THE MAN AND THE DOG

Prophet Muhammad ﷺ said: Once a man was walking down the road. The man got very thirsty and he came to a well. He went to the well and had a long drink. When he was leaving, he saw a dog who was tired and thirsty. The man remembered how thirsty he felt before he drank, and he knew that the dog must have felt the same way.

The man went down the well, filled his shoe with water and helped the dog drink. Allah forgave all of the man's sins, gave him many hasanat and rewards, and promised him Jannah.

THE WOMAN AND THE CAT

Prophet Muhammad ﷺ told us another story about a woman who trapped a cat.

The woman did not give the cat food to eat. She did not let the cat go out to look for food.

The woman kept the cat inside until it died. Allah ﷻ was very angry with the woman, and He promised she would go to Hellfire.

WORDS OF WISDOM
(Hadeeth Shareef)

حديث شريف

Narrated By Bukhari

عن عائشة رضي الله عنها: قال رسول الله ﷺ :
"إنَّ اللّهَ رَفيقٌ يُحِبُّ الرِّفْقَ في الأَمْرِ كُلّهِ"

TRANSLITERATION

"Inna-Allaha Rafeequn yuhibb-ur-rifqa fil-amri kullih."

TRANSLATION

Ai'sha (R) reported that the Prophet ﷺ said: "Allah is gentle. He loves kindness in every matter."

I want to be like the man who helped the dog and had all his bad deeds erased!

Me too! We should always be kind to people, animals, and plants, so we can go to Jannah too! Muslims should always be kind!

healthy habit

Be kind to people, animals, plants, and other things.
Do not harm them.
Take care of them.

study questions

1. How does Allah want us to act with our parents, friends, plants and animals?

2. What is a name of Allah that means He is Kind?

3. What is a good way to treat an animal?

4. What is a bad way to treat an animal?

5. Should we step on or hurt flowers and good plants?

Ithaar and Caring

questions?

1. Have you ever given away something you like to somebody else?
2. What can you do to show kindness to others?
3. How will we be rewarded if we care about each other?

word watch

[Al-Kawthar   الكوثر
    Ithaar   إيثار]

Helping the Poor

One day, Zaid and his classmates wanted to help their poor brothers and sisters around the world. They began collecting money in cans. Teacher Hibah told each student to call his or her can "My Kawthar Can."

Bilal asked Teacher Hibah: What is Al-Kawthar?

Teacher Hibah answered: It is a special river in Paradise (Jannah) that was given to our beloved Prophet Muhammad ﷺ by Allah ﷻ.

Mona: Why is Al-Kawthar river so special?

Al-Kawthar river is special for two reasons:

1 The Prophet ﷺ himself will give you a drink from the river on the Day of Judgment!!!

2 Its water is whiter than milk and sweeter than honey!!!

The students collected the coins. They hoped Allah would let them drink from **Al-Kawthar** because they were sharing their money. Zaid took money from his allowance and put it in the cans.

We call this Ithaar.

Ithaar is when you give away something you love to someone else who needs it.

When you practice **Ithaar**, you please Allah ﷻ, and your heart feels happy.

WORDS OF WISDOM
Holy Qur'an

سورة الكوثر
Surat-ul-Kawthar

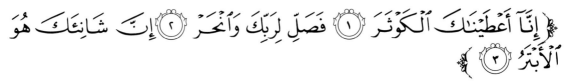

بِسْمِ إِنَّا أَعْطَيْنَاكَ ٱلْكَوْثَرَ ﴿١﴾ فَصَلِّ لِرَبِّكَ وَٱنْحَرْ ﴿٢﴾ إِنَّ شَانِئَكَ هُوَ ٱلْأَبْتَرُ ﴿٣﴾

TRANSLITERATION

[1] Inna a'taynak-al-kawthar
[2] Fasalli lirabbika wanhar
[3] Inna shani'aka huwa-al-abtar

TRANSLATION

[1] Indeed, We have granted you [Oh Muhammad], al-Kawthar
[2] So pray to your Lord and sacrifice [to Him alone].
[3] Indeed, your enemy is the one who will be forgotten.

Listen to the recitation of this sura, recite it and memorize it.

Zaid and his friends collected the money with love and care. In one month, the students collected about 95 cans full of coins!!!

Teacher Hibah was very happy and proud that her students were so kind and caring.

Leena Gives Up Her Bed

Leena's Aunt and Uncle and three cousins were coming from another country to visit for the summer. Leena was very excited. She helped her parents prepare the house for the visit. She helped set up mattresses for her cousins, but she knew her bed would be more comfortable to sleep on. She told her parents that she wanted to give up her bed for her cousins.

Mama: Why, Leena?

Leena: I want to practice Ithaar, and I want Allah ﷻ to reward me!

Mama was very proud of Leena.

WORDS OF WISDOM
Hadeeth Shareef

حديث شريف

Narrated By Muslim, Bukhari & Ahmad

عن أنس رضي الله عنه أن رسول الله ﷺ قال:
"لا يُؤْمِنُ أحَدكم حتى يحب لأخيه ما يحب لنفسه."

TRANSLITERATION

"La yo'minu Ahadakum hatta yuhibba li akheehi ma yuhibbu linafsih."

TRANSLATION

Anas reported that the Prophet ﷺ said:
"You will not truly believe until one wishes for his brother what he wishes for himself."

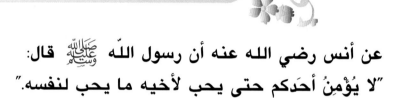

healthy
habit

Always care about others, especially the needy. Try to practice Ithaar all the time.

ACTIVITY time

You and your classmates can start your own "Can of Kawthar" using clean cans. Try to collect a good amount of money, and give it to the poor and the orphans.

study

questions

1. What does Ithaar mean?

2. If you are selfish, would you be practicing Ithaar?

3. Why is Al-Kawthar special?

4. Why did Leena give up her bed for her cousins?

5. Write down three ways you can show that you care for others.

I Obey My Parents

questions?

1 Who takes care of you at home?
2 Do you obey and care for him/her/them?
3 Why should you listen to your parents?
4 Who knows more, you or your parents?
5 Who knows even more than your parents?

word watch

Birrul Walidayn بِرِّ الوالدين

Mama watched Bilal run by.

Mama: Bilal, did you wash your hands?

Bilal: No, Mama, not yet.

Mama: You know you should wash your hands when you come home, dear. Remember to put your back-pack in your room.

healthy habit

Always keep yourself clean and put your things in place. This makes Allah and your parents happy.

Bilal really wanted to go outside and play basketball, but he knew it was more important to listen to Mama.

He wanted to show that he loved her.

Bilal: Okay, Mama!!!

He picked up his backpack and took it to his room, and then he washed his hands.

Later on in the evening, Bilal was helping Mama in the kitchen with Sarah. He was so hungry! He opened a cabinet and took out some cookies.

He was just about to take a bite, and Sarah saw him.

Sarah: "Bilal, it's almost dinner time. Baba says we shouldn't eat sweets right before dinner!"

But Bilal was so hungry!

Bilal: Sarah, I'll just eat one cookie. Please?

Mama: Bilal, if you eat a cookie now, then you won't be able to finish your dinner! Besides, dinner is better for you than a cookie. That's why Baba says to wait for dessert.

At the dinner table, Mama smiled at Bilal.

Mama: Bilal has been a very good boy today. He listened to me and obeyed Baba even when he wanted to do something else.

Bilal: Because I know you tell me what is good for me!

Baba: This is **Birrul Walidayn** that the Prophet ﷺ taught us.

Bilal: What is **Birrul Walidayn**, Dad?

Baba: It means obeying your parents and being kind to them. I used to obey my parents when I was young, and I still do. Allah ordered us to do so.

Mama: Also, when you obey your parents, you will make less mistakes, and all of us will be safe and happy.

Bilal and Sarah: We will always obey and respect you, Dad and Mom.

Our parents know more than us. We should listen to them.

Mama and Dad love us so much, Sarah! They tell us good things!

When we listen to our parents, we make Allah ﷻ happy.

healthy
habit

Always obey your parents, and do what they ask you to do before anything else. This makes Allah and your parents happy. The whole family will be happy too.

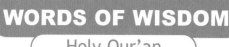

سورة الإسراء

Surat-ul-Israa': Ayah 23

﴾ وَقَضَىٰ رَبُّكَ أَلَّا تَعْبُدُوٓا۟ إِلَّآ إِيَّاهُ وَبِٱلْوَٰلِدَيْنِ إِحْسَٰنًا إِمَّا يَبْلُغَنَّ عِندَكَ ٱلْكِبَرَ أَحَدُهُمَآ أَوْ كِلَاهُمَا فَلَا تَقُل لَّهُمَآ أُفٍّ وَلَا تَنْهَرْهُمَا وَقُل لَّهُمَا قَوْلًا كَرِيمًا ﴿٢٣﴾ ﴿

TRANSLITERATION

"Waqada rabbuka alla ta'budoo illa iyyahu wabilwali-dayni i hsana, imma yablughanna 'indak-al-kibara ahaduhuma aw kilahuma fala taqul lahuma offiw-wala tanharhuma waqul lahuma qawlan kareema."

TRANSLATION

"Your Lord has decreed that you worship no one but Him, and that you be kind to parents. Whether one or both of them become old in your life, do not say to them a word of contempt, nor shout at them, but talk to them in a polite way."

Listen to the recitation of this sura, recite it and memorize it.

حديث شريف

Narrated By Abu Dawood

عن معاوية بن حيدة: قال يا رسول الله من أبر، قال: أمك ثم أمك ثم أمك ثم أباك ثم الأقرب فالأقرب"

رواه أبو داود

TRANSLITERATION

"Mu'awiyah: Man Abarr? The Prophet: Ummak, thumma ummak, thumma ummak, thumma abak, thumm-al-aqrab fal-aqrab."

TRANSLATION

Mu'awiyah Ibn Haydah asked the Prophet ﷺ : Whom should I treat best? He said: "Your mother, your mother, your mother, and your father. Then your relatives."

study

questions

1 How did Bilal obey and listen to his parents?

2 Why did Mama ask Bilal to clean up before playing basketball?

3 Why did Baba say to wait until after dinner to eat sweets?

4 Who do we make happy if we are good children?

5 Who will be kind to you if you are kind to your parents? What should you do if you disobey your parents?

I Am A Muslim, I Must Be Clean

questions?

1 Why must Muslims be clean?
2 What different things do you keep clean?
3 How do you help clean at home?

word watch

Taharah   طهارة
Najasah   نجاسة
Al-Jumu'ah   الجُمعة

Taharah   is purity and cleanliness.

Najasah   means dirty, or impure.

They are opposites. A Muslim should always practice Taharah.

حديث شريف

Narrated By Muslim

عن أبي مالك الأشعري رضي الله عنه: قال رَسولُ الله ﷺ :
"الطَّهور شَطْر الإيمانْ."

TRANSLITERATION

"At-Tahooru Shatr-ul-Iman"

TRANSLATION

Abu Malik reported that the Prophet ﷺ said:
"Purity is half of faith."

I keep Myself clean

I love to take showers so that I smell nice and stay healthy.

We should especially take showers on Fridays because **Al-Jumu'ah** is a special day for Muslims.

I always wear clean clothes so that I look nice and neat.

Allah ﷻ said:

"Wa-thiyabaka fatahhir."
It means: "And purify your clothes." (74:4)

When I go to the bathroom I wash myself and my hands. I make sure to keep my clothes clean from **Najasah**. I keep the bathroom clean, too!

I brush my teeth and comb my hair.

Allah loves for our mouths to smell fresh when we pray. The Prophet ﷺ used a siwak to keep his teeth clean all the time.

I keep my House clean

I clean up after myself and put my things in place.

I keep my Masjid clean

I keep my School clean

I keep my Earth clean

s t u d y

questions

1. What does Taharah mean? What is the opposite?

2. What are some things you do to make yourself clean?

3. How do you help keep your home clean?

4. What are other places you can think of to keep clean?

5. What did the Prophet ﷺ say about purity or cleanliness.

A Dinner in Our Neighbor's Home

questions?

1. Do you ever go to your friend's house for dinner?
2. What do you do there?
3. How can you be a good guest?

word watch

Yameen يـمين
Shimal شِمال

"Leena and Zaid, we are going to Bilal's house for dinner on Friday, InshaAllah," said their mother. Leena and Zaid jumped up and down because they were very excited!

They were smiling from ear to ear!

Bilal and Sarah were very excited too! At school, Bilal told Zaid about the games they were going to play together.

Bilal said: "First we'll eat dinner, and then we can play all night long! We'll have a blast!"

He had the plan all figured out.

"We can play Race to Al-Ka'bah!" Leena and Sarah said at the same time. They just had to wait until tomorrow!

Friday finally came! Zaid's father woke him up for fajr, and he jumped out of bed!

Zaid and Leena went to school. At home, even baby Yusuf was excited!

After school, Leena and Zaid started getting ready for dinner. Then they heard their father's voice, "Are we ready to go?"

Zaid and Leena ran downstairs. When everyone sat down in the car, Leena started to recite the traveling dua'a, and the whole family joined in.

healthy
habits

When you leave home say:

"بسم الله، توكلنا على الله، لا حول ولا قوة إلا بالله."

" Bismillah, tawakkalna alAllah, la hawla wala quwwata
illa billah"

It means: In the name of Allah, we rely on Allah, we have
no power without Allah.

When you enter the house say:

"بسم الله ولجنا، وبسم الله خرجنا، اللهم إنا نسألك خير المولج وخير المخرج."

"Bismillahi walajna, wa-bismillahi kharajna, allahuma
inna nas'alula khayr-al-mawloj wa khayr-al-makhraj"

It means: With the name of Allah we enter, and with the
name of Allah we exit. Oh Allah we ask You a good entering
and a good exit.

★★★★★★★★★★★★★★★★★★★★★★

**Learn to say this dua'a when you are leaving to go
somewhere:**

"سبحان الذي سخر لنا هذا وما كنا له مُقرِنين وإنَّا إلى ربنا لمنقلبون."

"Subhan-Allathi Sakhara lana hatha wa ma kunna
lahu muqrineen wa inna ila rabbina lamunqaliboon."

It means: Glory be to Allah who made this (car)
available to us. And we will not worship others with
Him. We are all returning to Allah in the Hereafter.

Finally, they reached Bilal's house! Zaid ran to ring the doorbell. Bilal answered the door.

"Assalamu alaykum!!!" Bilal said.
"Wa alaykum assalaam!!" said Zaid's Family.
The children all said, "Let's go play!"

Bilal's parents welcomed Zaid's family.
Everyone was smiling!

After a while, dinner was ready.
Bilal's Mom said: "Okay kids, go wash up before we eat dinner."
All the children went to wash their hands and mouths.

Everyone sat down at the table. Zaid was so hungry! Bilal's mother asked if everyone said their dua'a to thank Allah before they ate.

healthy
h a b i t

Always say this dua'a before you eat:

"اللهم بارك لنا في ما رزقتنا وقنا عذاب النّار، بسم الله."

"Allahumma barik lana feema razaqtana wa-qina athab-an-nar, bismillah."

This means: "Oh Allah! Bless (the food) You gave us and save us from the punishment of the hellfire.   In the name of Allah."

WORDS OF WISDOM

Hadeeth Shareef

حديث شريف

Narrated by Al-Bukhari and Muslim

عن عمر بن أبي سلمة رضي الله عنه: قال لي رسول الله ﷺ :
"يا غلام، سمِّ الله وكل بيمينك وكل مما يليك."

رواه البخاري ومسلم

TRANSLITERATION

"Ya Ghulam sammillah, wa-kul biyameenik, wa kul mimma yaleek."

TRANSLATION

Omar Ibn Abi Salamah reported that the Prophet ﷺ said: "Oh Boy, Say Allah's Name, (i.e., say Bismillah before starting eating), eat with your right hand, and eat from what is near you."

Zaid began to get silly. He took some of his mashed potatoes and put them on Bilal's nose! They were giggling! Bilal tried to do it back to Zaid, and he accidentally spilled his father's drink!

The boys weren't laughing anymore. Zaid's mother asked them to stop playing with their food. The boys cleaned up the mess, and they promised not to do this mistake again.

Leena wanted to drink all of her juice at once. She was drinking with her left hand. Her father kindly told her, "The Prophet taught us to drink one sip at a time, and not to finish our cup in less than three sips." Also, He taught us to eat and drink with our yameen (right hand) not our shimal (our left hand).

Zaid, Sarah, Bilal, and Leena's parents were very happy that the children did not waste their food.

After they finished eating, the families began to say the dua'a of finishing a meal. This time, Zaid's father told everyone what it meant.

Zaid and Leena smiled at Bilal's mother and said, "Jazakum-ullahu Khayran for your yummy food!"

It was a nice thing to say!

healthy
h a b i t

Say this dua'a after you finish eating:

"الحمد لله الذي أطعمنا وسقانا وجعلنا مسلمين."

"Al-Hamdulillah al-lathi at'amana wa saqana wa ja'alana Muslimeen."

This means, "All praise is due to Allah (SWT) who gave us food and drink and made us Muslims."

Bilal's mother replied: "Wa Iyyakum, Leena and Zaid. We are all glad you came!"

When everyone was getting up, Leena, Zaid, and Bilal noticed that the mothers were clearing the table. They wanted to help too! It would show their mothers that they were thankful for the dinner.

After dinner the children played some more, but then it was time to go.

Zaid's Dad called the children.

"It's time to go, let's get our shoes on."

Zaid and Leena did not want to leave, but they knew it was important to listen to their parents.

Bilal's family thanked their guests for coming. "Jazakum Allahu khairan for having us!" Leena and Zaid said.

"Wa iyyakum!" Bilal's parents said.

Everyone said "Assalamu Alaykum," and said good-bye to a fun night!

healthy

habit

Always be very polite when you are at other people's houses.

study

questions

1 What should you say when you meet a Muslim brother or sister?

2 What should you do and say before and after you eat?

3 Which hand should you eat with? Why?

4 Is it a good idea to play with your food? What can happen if you play with your food?

5 How can you show that you are thankful to your parents?

questions?

1 What should we do when an elder tells us to do something?
2 What are some things you need to do before going to bed?
3 What is the best way to sleep?
4 What is the first thing you should do in the morning?

word watch

Al-Mu'awwithat المُعَوِّذاتْ

Leena and Zaid loved visiting their grandparents. They used to wait for the holidays to come, so Mama and Dad would take them over to their grandparents' house. Leena and Zaid slept over there on vacations. They were always excited to be with their grandparents.

On Eid day, everyone visited the grandparents' house. They enjoyed eating dinner together and sharing stories. When Leena and Zaid's parents left, they stayed to spend the night!!!

When bedtime came, Leena and Zaid did not want to go to bed. They wanted to hear more stories from their grandparents. Leena and Zaid's grandmother said, "We will finish our stories in the morning. Now it is time to go to bed." Leena and Zaid obeyed their grandmother right away.

They brushed their teeth.

They put on their pajamas.

They hugged and said good-night to their grandparents.

Leena and Zaid's grandmother tucked them into bed, and reminded them to say their dua'a.

Their grandmother also reminded them of Ayat-ul-Kursi and Al-Mu'awwithat, which are **Surat-ul-Falaq** and **Surat-un-Nas**. The dua'a and Al-Qur'an are protection for us from Shaytan.

Leena, Zaid, and their grandmother said the dua'a and the suwar all together. Leena and Zaid kissed their grandmother goodnight and gave her a big hug.

When grandmother was leaving the room, she noticed Leena and Zaid were about to sleep on their stomachs. She told them how Prophet Muhammad ﷺ taught us that it is better to sleep on our right side or our back. Leena and Zaid thanked their grandmother for teaching them that.

healthy
habit

1. Memorize this dua'a and say it every night before you go to sleep.

"بِاسْمِكَ اللّهُمَّ أَمُوتُ وأَحيا."

"Bissmika Allahumma Amoutu Wa Ahya."

It means:"By Your Name, Oh Allah, I die and live."

2. Read Ayatul-Kursi and Al-Mu'awwithat before you sleep too.

ACTIVITY time

Make a checklist that you can use before you go to bed. Here's an idea of how it can look:

BEDTIME TASK	DONE?
1 Say "Assalamu Alaykum, goodnight" to your parents	○
2 Change your clothes	○
3 Brush your teeth	○
4 Make Wudoo'	○
5 Pray Isha	○
6 Say your dua'a and Mu'awwithat	○
7 Sleep on your right side	○
8 Close your eyes	○

Allah 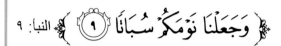 made the night so we can rest our bodies and minds. Allah said in the Qur'an,

﴿ وَجَعَلْنَا نَوْمَكُمْ سُبَاتًا ﴿٩﴾ ﴾ النبأ: ٩

"And We made your sleep for rest."

Sleeping is a gift from Allah.

Allah ﷻ made the day so we can work and learn. Allah said in the Qur'an:

﴿ وَجَعَلْنَا ٱلنَّهَارَ مَعَاشًا ﴿١١﴾ ﴾ النبأ: ١١

"And We made the day for livelihood."

When you wake up in the morning, you should thank Allah ﷻ for giving you another day.

At Fajr time, Leena and Zaid's grandparents woke them up to pray. They were very proud of them for doing a great job in salah.

After breakfast, Leena and Zaid's grandparents finished their stories as they had promised. Soon, Mama and Dad came to pick them up. Leena and Zaid thanked their grandparents with a hug and a kiss for taking such good care of them, and they all said, "Assalamu Alaykum!"

healthy habit

Be a morning person. Sleep early to wake up early. Start your day early at Fajr time and sleep right after Isha' time.

healthy habit

When you wake up in the morning, say:

''الحمد للّه الذي أحيانا بعد ما أماتنا وإليه النشور.''

"Al-Hamdu lillah-il-lathi ahyana ba'da ma amatana wa-ilayh-in-nushoor."

It means: "Praise be to Allah for giving us life after death, and to Him we will return."

WORDS OF WISDOM

Holy Qur'an

المعوذات

Al-Mu'awwithat

قُلْ أَعُوذُ بِرَبِّ ٱلْفَلَقِ ۝ مِن شَرِّ مَا خَلَقَ ۝ وَمِن شَرِّ غَاسِقٍ إِذَا وَقَبَ ۝ وَمِن شَرِّ ٱلنَّفَّـٰثَـٰتِ فِى ٱلْعُقَدِ ۝ وَمِن شَرِّ حَاسِدٍ إِذَا حَسَدَ ۝

قُلْ أَعُوذُ بِرَبِّ ٱلنَّاسِ ۝ مَلِكِ ٱلنَّاسِ ۝ إِلَـٰهِ ٱلنَّاسِ ۝ مِن شَرِّ ٱلْوَسْوَاسِ ٱلْخَنَّاسِ ۝ ٱلَّذِى يُوَسْوِسُ فِى صُدُورِ ٱلنَّاسِ ۝ مِنَ ٱلْجِنَّةِ وَٱلنَّاسِ ۝

TRANSLITERATION

[1] Qul a'oothu birabb-il-falaq
[2] Min sharri ma khalaq
[3] Wamin sharri ghasiqin itha waqab
[4] Wamin sharr-in-naffathati fil-'uqad
[5] Wamin sharri hasidin itha hasad

---

[1] Qul a'oothu birabb-in-nas
[2] Malik-in-nas
[3] Ilah-in-nas
[4] Min sharr-il-waswas-il-khannasi
[5] Allathee yuwaswisu fee sudoor-in-nas
[6] Min aljinnati wannas

TRANSLATION

[1] Say: I seek protection of the Lord of the Dawn,
[2] From the evil of created things;
[3] From the evil of Darkness as it overspreads;
[4] From the evil of those who blow into the knots (practicing magic);
[5] And from the evil of the envious one as he practices envy.

---

[1] Say: I seek protection of the Lord of Mankind,
[2] The King (or Ruler) of Mankind,
[3] The God (or Judge) of Mankind,
[4] From the evil of the whisperer (of Evil), who withdraws (after his whisper),
[5] (The same) who whispers into the hearts of mankind,
[6] Among jinns and among men.

Listen to the recitation of this sura, recite it and memorize it.

questions

1 Did Leena and Zaid obey their grandmother when she said it was time for bed? What do you learn from that?

2 What dua'a and suwar did their grandmother remind them to say before they slept?

3 Is it good to sleep on your stomach? What is the best way to sleep?

4 Why did Allah create night? Why did He create day?

5 What is the first thing you should say when you wake up?

INDEX